Organizational Effectiveness Simplified for Human Resource Professionals

Abi Alade

Copyright © 2021 by Abimbola Alade
All rights reserved. No portion of this book is permitted to be reproduced, stored for later retrieval or transmitted in any form, by any means, recording, mechanical, scanning, electronic, photocopying or otherwise without express permission from the author.
The content of this book is for informational, educational and entertainment purposes only and by no means is the author making any guarantees.

Table of Contents

Introduction --5
Strategy --6
Processes ---7
Structure and job design --7
Human resource practices-- 8
Culture -- 9
Organizational Culture ---10
How do we Recognize Organizational Culture ----------------------------------11
Types of Organizational Culture ---12
Changing Organization Culture ---16
Keys to a Successful Culture Shift --- 16
Organizational Structure ---18
Types of Organizational Structures --18
Symptoms of Organization Design Problem -------------------------------------19
Team Dynamics --22
Types of Teams --22
Stages of Team Development --23
Conflict in a Team --26
Identifying Team Dynamics ---28
Team Interventions --30
Team Members Competencies and Capabilities ----------------------------------32
Employee Engagement -- 35

History of Employee Engagement: Scientific Management -------------- 36
History of Employee Engagement: Motivation & Satisfaction --------- 38

Employee Engagement: Since the 1990s ----------------------------- 41
Models of Employee Engagement ----------------------------------- 42
Drivers of Employee Engagement ---------------------------------- 46

Change Management --- 48

Reactions to Change -- 49
How to Lead Change Management: Lewin's Model --------------------- 49
How to Lead Change Management: Kotter's 8 Steps ------------------ 50
How to Lead Change Management: The Action Research Model --------- 52
How to Lead Change Management: Positive Change Model ------------- 52
Organizational Learning -- 53
Change Management Tools -- 54
Communicating a Change Activity ---------------------------------- 55
Interferences to Communication ----------------------------------- 57
How to Ensure Effective Communication ---------------------------- 59
How to Improve Communication Channels ---------------------------- 60

Introduction

Usually, when I am faced with an aspect of a practice such as human resources, I wonder, why do we have to do this? How does this fit in into the whole picture? So, *why study organizational effectiveness?* It is because human resource professionals (HRPs) do not operate in a vacuum, they work within organizations. Their work, programs, and projects are targeted at driving the organization's proficiency and performance. It is important to know that management is all about effectively meeting organizations' goals, and that would be a recurring theme in this text. *What is organizational effectiveness?* I have two definitions here; one of them is that it is the total skills or all of the skills that involve HRPs being able to use the tools that they have to optimize an organization's performance, as they implement the organizational strategy. So, HRPs are using certain tools that they have to efficiently maximize the use of the resources within the organization – people/ human resources included so that organizations can meet their goals. The second definition is, organizational effectiveness is about aligning strategy, processes, structure & job design, and organizational personality, also known as the organizational culture with HRPs' practices. Because HRPs are using the tools that they have, HRPs have a manner in which they want to achieve these goals. Thus, they use set programs to achieve these for the organization, which involves aligning their practices and those programs with organizational strategy, processes, structure and job design, and the culture of the organization.

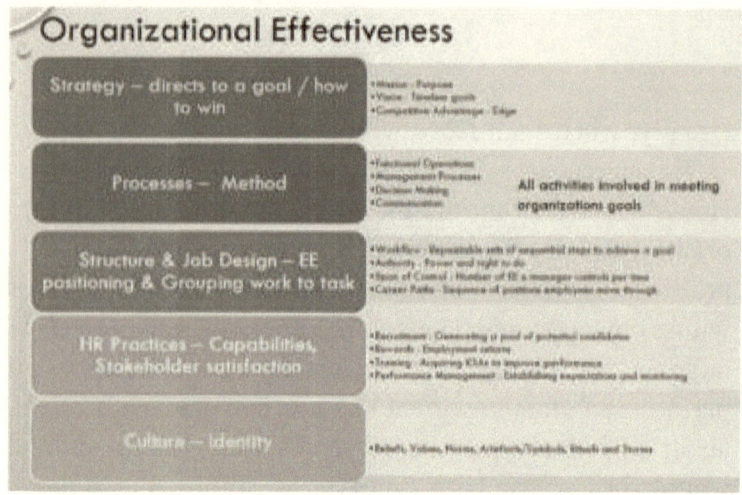

So, *what is strategy?* It is the direction to a goal; how the organization wants to win. It involves the mission, vision, and competitive advantage.

What are processes? A process is a method of doing something.

What does structure & job design mean? It is the positioning of employees and grouping of work into tasks.

What are HR Practices? They are HRPs' capabilities as it involves stakeholder satisfaction.

What is culture? It means identity.

We said organizational effectiveness is aligning all these main topics with the organization's strategy, now let's go into details so we can know what elements HRPs align with organizational strategy.

Strategy is how the organization wants to win and It involves;

1. **The mission** of an organization is its purpose - why does the organization exist? You hear people in conversations say things like, what's your mission here?

What's your purpose here? It is the same thing with organizations.

2. **Vision** is a timeless goal. The vision for an organization is like a never-ending state that they continue to strive for. If an organization has achieved its vision, I don't believe there's any reason for the organization to continue existing. That is why it is timeless. It consists of a series of goals that the organization needs to continue fulfilling, to be in existence.

3. **Competitive advantage** is the edge an organization has over its competitors.

Processes are the methods of the organization that HRPs align with strategy. It involves;

1. **Functional operations,**
2. **Management processes,**
3. **Decision making, and**
4. **Communication.**

That is every activity that is involved in meeting organizational goals.

Structure and job design is the design of the organization and it includes workflow, authority, the span of control, and career paths.

1. **Workflow** is a repeatable set of sequential steps to achieve a goal. For example, we want to carry a pen from one place to another, how do we do that? It could be 1. Lift the pen, maybe use a machine or a tool, then 2. Press a button that will move that machine, and then 3. Drop the pen where it's supposed to be. Workflow is a repeatable set of

sequential steps to achieve a goal - I'm thinking of manufacturing here, a repeatable set of steps that are taken to manufacture whatever it is that a company is processing.

2. **Authority** is the power and right to do, given to someone in charge; a supervisor, manager, or anyone that is in charge of resources including human resources.

3. **A span of control** is the number of employees that a manager has authority over per time.

4. **Career paths** are a sequence of positions employees move through within the organization. A career path for, maybe a junior staff in a position, then after a while, they get to the next position, up until the peak of their career in that organization, if they end up staying there until retirement. So it's a position or several sequences of positions that an employee occupies from the time they get into an organization, to the time that they leave.

Human resource practices. We are well familiar with these. HRPs engage in other disciplines such as recruitment, rewards - total rewards or compensation, training, and performance management. Human resource practices in this case include;

1. **Recruitment** is generating a pool of potential candidates when an organization is looking for a particular skill and then creating an advertisement so people can apply. The potential candidate that will take the job is in that pool. That's recruitment.

2. A **reward** is employment returns that employees get for the services that they render.

3. **Training** is acquiring knowledge, skills, and the ability to improve performance within an organization.

4. **Performance management** is not just measuring employees' performance but establishing what the expectations are, and then measuring the employees against those set expectations.

Culture is the beliefs of an organization's values, norms, artifacts or symbols, rituals, and stories that exist within and are unique to the organization. Stories like, "Oh, this is how this happened" or "This is the story of how this organization was formed," or "This is why this happened." This is similar to stories that you pass on from one generation of employees to the next as to why they do things a certain way.

Organizational Culture

Organizational culture is the recognizable identity of an organization. Just like human beings, culture is the personality of the organization. It is what makes an organization different from another, or the similarities between an organization and another organization. How people are similar or how people are different, it's the same thing with organizations. An organization's culture is influenced by beliefs and assumptions. And it comes from what people hear, what people observe, what people learn, what has been tried before, what works and what doesn't work. And when things don't work out, there needs to be a rethink. Organizational culture is the foundation for teams - when a new person joins an organization, the culture is taught to them. It is how things are done within the organization, it influences the attitude of employees that work within an organization. It is about what people believe, as everybody in an organization should have a common goal, a common ground, a common factor that brings everyone together. Culture is formed by what people hear; it is the ideal way that things should be done. For example, what did the founders envision before they founded the company? What was their ideal situation for the organization? - How things will be done. Culture usually grows with experience. It is changeable but should be stable enough to support strategy for positive results.

So, organizational effectiveness, once again, is aligning strategy, culture, processes, structure, and job design, with HRPs' practices. For there to be positive results in an organization (for an organization to meet its goal), culture should support strategy, or the strategy should support culture for positive results; and that is where the HR professional comes in, hence the importance of this discipline in human resources management. In the same breath, we have ***Organizational Climate,*** which is employees' perception. So, culture is ideally the way things should be done, but is that how the employees perceive it, is that how they feel? For example, management can say we love and care for our employees, but in reality, is that what is going on? Is that how employees perceive it? Because the managers or leadership can say that "this is our culture, this is what we do," but employees don't see it that way. So how employees feel about how they are being treated, that's organizational climate. Climate influences emotions, it influences how employees feel. It is the actual way that things are done, not just the ideal way now. Management can have the ideal way in their mind, but in reality, how are things done, is it the same thing that management has envisioned? You can understand organizational climate by surveying employees, hearing from employees, and obtaining feedback, to see if culture and climate are on the same page. Organizational climate is dynamic and job satisfaction depends on what the employees feel. If an employee feels that they are valued, they will have job satisfaction, and that's basically what that means. Although organizational climate may not be the best initially, because it is dynamic, it can be changed once an HR professional in this case has that awareness and the task of balancing the organizational culture with organizational strategy.

How do we Recognize Organizational Culture? By **observing symbols within organizations or artifacts** – a physical manifestation of their beliefs, like translating it into physical form. One example that comes to mind is Nando's (don't judge me :)) In Nando's, one of their main products is the grilled chicken, and everything you see around has to do with chickens. They also serve corn on the cob, which is used to feed chickens, and their salt shaker is in the shape of an egg (chicken egg). Their table number is on a Nando's chicken table stick, which also is in the shape of a chicken. That is a typical example of symbols and artifacts for an organization that is translating their culture or what they are about into symbols.

We can also recognize organizational culture **by holding employee focus groups** and conducting **employee surveys** - these can let us in on the organizational climate.

Examining core behaviors - What main behaviors are exhibited in an organization? That's another way to recognize organizational culture. Also, **how does the organization make decisions?** You can have an incline into the culture by examining how the organization makes decisions. What **communication styles and channels** are used by the organization? What are their **reward structures?** How do they reward their employees? If you look at the **organization's structure** as well, - which we'll be talking about later. You can have an inkling into what the culture is if you **assess the nature of relationships in an organization**. Are the people friendly, or is everyone minding their business? Understanding the **leadership style** within an organization is another way to understand the culture.

Types of Organizational Culture
There are four basic culture types: Clan, Adhocracy, Hierarchy, and Market.

For **Clan**, the culture is family-oriented, people-oriented, and friendly. They want to know your family, and they want to know you personally; it has a family feel. They even want to see pictures of your relatives. So it is okay for you to display such in the office. In some organizations, you can bring your pets, and that's something you can see in a Clan organization culture. The leadership serves as mentors; they are very involved, serving as drivers, mentors to the employees, or as guardians to their employees. They value participation, commitment, and communication, and they believe human development and participation lead to effectiveness.

Adhocracy is very entrepreneurial. I see this as a goal-getting organization. Leaders are the ones foremost in everything, showing the employees how things are done. They are innovators, visionaries, and entrepreneurs. For example, IT startups. Although it's no longer a startup, when I think of startups, I think of Silicon Valley companies; Facebook, and the likes of them. The leaders value change and they have to have the ability to change quickly because they have to make a profit and remain in the market. They are always changing to avoid losing market relevance. They believe in creativity, innovation, new resources, and that these produce effectiveness.

Market - they just believe in results. The Market culture is a competitive one. Leadership drives people hard. There are several examples of companies that have the market culture; we don't want to name names here. Employees complain that an average staff is overworked. They just believe in being market leaders, almost like, "We are not keen on how we affect employees." They believe in achieving their goals, making a profit, and believe that effectiveness is focusing on the customer and competing aggressively. So to an organization that has a market culture type, if they don't see competitiveness in employees, aggressive competition, and feel employees are not focused on the customer, they don't believe that they are being effective.

Hierarchy The hierarchy culture type is a structured environment. The leaders are the coordinators. They are the monitors, and they organize everything. They value efficiency and consistency and doing everything on time. If there was a temperament to it, I would say its melancholy. They stick to the plan and arrangements. They want everything to be done uniformly, and they want everything to go according to plan. They do not value creativity; "don't bring creativity here." It would be frustrating for an employee who believes in letting their creativity shine through their work, to work in an organization that does not believe in that. They believe that people should follow rules, and they appreciate it when people follow rules. They believe that effectiveness is when control exists in an organization.

4 Basic Culture Types

	Flexible Structure	
Internal Focus	CLAN (Family)	ADHOCRACY (Entrepreneurial)
	HIERARCHY (Structured)	MARKET (Results)
	Stable Structure	External Focus

In this pictorial representation of the culture types, clan and adhocracy have a **flexible structure.** The clan culture type is family-oriented. They are not hard about anything and are very caring. An employee could say, "Oh, I don't feel well today" or "my dog died"; they are flexible. Adhocracy is entrepreneurial. As long as people are delivering on their tasks, they don't care about how it is done; they believe in innovation - So that's flexibility.

Although, adhocracy, is entrepreneurial - because every company is in business to make a profit, It is similar to market culture in that they are both results-oriented. Hence, the market and adhocracy culture are **externally focused.**

Now again, the market culture, because it's all about the market share and profit, still values a **stable structure,** and they have that in common with the hierarchy structure because companies want to know where the profit will come from. Can we at least have a little bit of certainty? No business wants to be in the dark. Now the clan and hierarchy culture types are **internally focused.** The hierarchy culture type is internally focused in the sense that they are particular about how the people within the organization behave. They want orderliness, nothing extreme, no outliers; everybody just following the rules. The clan culture is also internally focused, in the sense that they are focused on every single person that works in that organization. Organizations need to choose from the four since they cannot practice all four culture types efficiently. However, a blend of two is possible but one is most dominant. Let's bear in mind that we are talking about culture because HRPs need to understand the culture to be able to align it with the organizations' strategy.

Changing Organization Culture
If it is identified that an organization's culture is not the best, then there is a need for a culture shift. Organizations need to know where they are - What's the current culture? What is the preferred culture, and if the current culture is not working, what are the gaps that exist between the current culture and the preferred culture? Also, what needs to be done to take the organization to the preferred culture? That is a culture shift.

Keys to a Successful Culture Shift
For there to be a successful culture shift, an organization's leadership must be devoted. We've seen the roles of leadership in an organization's culture previously, where we talked about the organization's leadership being innovators in Adhocracy. So for there to be a successful culture shift, leadership needs to play a major role.

There needs to be **a clear strategic vision** - where is the organization going? It has been decided that there is a need to change the culture, so what would the new culture be like? And why is the culture changing? - clear strategic vision. Now, the **top management needs to be committed to change.** Management cannot be stuck in one way of thinking when the team is trying to be dynamic. They have to be in the lead for the culture shift.

There is a need to **review organization structure, processes, and HR programs**. HRPs should be focused on changing the old culture, to determine if there's a need to structure the organization in a certain way that would aid or be beneficial to the new culture. Also, if there's a need to change the organization's processes, HR programs will be the tool used to make that change happen.

Employee socialization is getting employees involved in the new culture that the organization is changing to. If employees are already used to a clan culture for example, and suddenly - the new culture involves innovation or competition, it might be too hard of an environment for some employees to work in. So for a culture change to be successful, the employees need to be carried along since it's a new way of life for them. And the expectation is for the current employees to induct the new joiners because as we said before, that culture is taught to new joiners. So if we're changing culture, we need the employees to give the culture "life," for it to be successfully passed to future employees. Another way to change culture is through **positive reinforcement.** Recurrently educating the organization as a whole is the destination. "This is what we are doing, and this is why we are doing it"; so that everybody imbibes the new culture.

Organizational Structure

Organizational structure provides the context in which a team performs. It is a design for how teams are going to perform, how activities are directed, and usually, an organizational structure is sometimes designed by skills, i.e. people that have the same set of skills are grouped by the business function that they serve, the process that they use to carry out their business, the kind of clients they have, or where they are located. So to expatiate on that, we have different types of team structures within organizations.

Types of Organizational Structures
We have a **functional structure** where employees are grouped because they have the same set of skills. They use the same tools and processes, and their department head reports to the president. So think of an organizational structure where every team has a head, head of human resources, head of information technology, head of finance, etc. And in the human resources group, the team reporting to the head of human resources are human resource people. They have the same skills, and they use the same tools and processes. Then it is the head of human resources that would report to the president of the organization.

In a **product or activity-based structure,** employees are grouped by departments, based on the activities that they perform or the product offerings. For example, you have a television team and a radio team in a communication outfit. So within that television team, there are human resource officers, and human resource officers of the radio team, depending on the product of the organization. The **client-based structure** is similar to the product structure, in the sense that employees are grouped only based on the kind of

clients they serve. For example, like clothing store departments, you have a department for kids, men, and women, depending on the client base. Within that client base, you may have children's customer service person etc.
The geographic structure is when employees are grouped based on where they are located. For example, employees are grouped by the geographical location they work out of, or they may represent eastern, western, southern, or northern regions, and it can be further broken down. In the geographic structure, you have the head of human resources leading the human resources team for the location; head of finance leading the finance team for the location, etc. It is these heads of teams that report to the president of the organization.
Matrix structure is like a cross-multiplication table. Employees are grouped based on two factors, maybe location or leadership of the department. It is a combination of structures; there are two bosses: project and function-based. So now think of a cross between the functional structure - everybody working together with the same skills and also based on geographical location. Teams are led by the location head and also the head of the functional area in which they operate.
Boundaryless structure is made up of small teams of employees formed and dissolved as necessary. It can be cross-functional or cross-level. For example, consulting organizations that just form teams to solve a problem or do a project. There are no boundaries, and it is very flexible and fluid across functions and levels in the organization.

Symptoms of Organization Design Problem
Organization designs are faulty when there are unclear roles, tasks, responsibilities; everyone is doing whatever they like, there is no balance between routine and innovation, and no

clear direction has been set; that is what you get when you have a symptom known as **bad job design.** Next to that is a **bad structural design.** The matrix structure is complex enough, now add another unique structure to the mix to make it even more complicated – what you get is a recipe for a confused team. Employees would be drawn in so many directions, reporting to multiple bosses, wondering about who to report to, whose authority is superior, who a project is to be delivered to, etc.

Ineffective spans of control we said spans of control are the number of people that report to a person in an organization. When you have someone that is supposed to manage maybe five people, managing about a hundred or more, there is a problem in organization design.

Insufficient information sharing when there are people in an organization who do not even know what is going on. When relevant information does not flow in their direction, and there is no clear information channel, then you know there is a break somewhere or the structure of the organization is faulty. **Duplication of efforts** can happen when everybody is doing whatever they feel like doing - bad job design. Someone would do a task that someone else completed minutes ago, efforts are duplicated, and there is no work schedule or specification; that is not healthy for any organization to have.

Then we have **departmental conflict.** When departments think that they are each other's enemies because a clear relationship has not been charted to let each department know how they fit into the organizational plan as a whole, and there is no sense of co-dependency. And lastly, when organizations have **too many committees,** it is a symptom of organization design problems. Think of any setup/organization or entity that you know that forms committees upon committees to investigate committees. Too many committees that are not creating anything.

And every one of these symptoms leads to organizational inefficiency. Organizations cannot fully function properly as they should, and until these problems are dealt with, there would be wasted resources, so many things slipping through the cracks, employee burnout with no productivity, etc.

Team Dynamics

Team dynamics are interactions within a team. How do team members interact with one another, and how does one team and all its members interact with other teams within the organization? So getting along essentially; that is team dynamics.

Types of Teams
There are different types of teams. There are **traditional work teams** - which are just action problem-solving teams. They meet a few times per week to problem-solve specific issues e.g. quality or efficiency improvement, but they do not implement. They only write a report, because they have solved the problem. And they leave it to the people that will implement it.

Employee involvement teams - employees are involved in making suggestions to whatever problem, challenge, task, or whatever the team has to do. The employee is involved in coming up with ideas and can make suggestions.

Semi-autonomous teams - these groups are cross-trained in different skills; they can almost work independently, as the name says. They can make decisions and solve problems concerning a process. However, they need approval, so that is where the semi-autonomous comes in; they are partially independent workgroups.

Self-managing teams - they are like construction workers. They have no boss, and every member is responsible for the aspect of their work. They can make decisions. For example, "it is raining, we cannot do this part of the construction today, and we will do it tomorrow." They manage themselves, and they know when to do their work. They know what problems they are facing concerning the work they are doing. They can make decisions concerning their work and require no management approval, which could lead to absenteeism at times.

Cross-functional teams - involve employees on the same level in the organization. They could also be transnational, maybe managers, from different functional areas to solve complex problems; they are task forces or committees. Team members are from, maybe finance, customer service, etc. For example, you are trying to design a system that would encompass all the processes that the organization goes through in providing service from start to finish. For example, maybe customer service is the one that would bring in the orders or guide employees to making the orders within that new system. So there is going to be an entry-level of bringing in the order, and then the finance team will be involved in how the payments should be made. So, you bring in members of the team from different individually unique teams to solve a complex problem.

Project teams - are created for one-time projects only, and they are led by project managers. Say we want to build a raft after that project is done. The team is done as well and they go back to their various teams.

Virtual teams - rely on technology; they are in different parts of the world. They hardly interact directly with one another, possibly because they only log on to their virtual meetings at scheduled times. It will be rare for there to be social interaction or any direct interaction apart from when they have to meet virtually. Virtual teams can develop into physical teams.

Stages of Team Development

There are four main stages of team development. For a team to work together efficiently, they will go through the four main different stages.

The first one is the **forming stage** where no one knows anyone yet i.e. team members do not know each other assuming they do not work together already in the same organization. Everyone is still trying to size up each other. "We don't know who you are, we don't know what this team is fully all about." "We just know a team called XYZ was created." Group members behave independently; "what exactly we are going to be doing in details, we don't know yet, but we are here. We are trying to smile, we are trying to be friendly, not to step on anyone's toes until we get to know each other." That is team forming. How long teams stay in this stage depends on how frequently the team meets. If the team meets every break time, five days a week, or once a month, that will determine how long the team will stay in the forming stage. If a group of people meets five times a week that is 20 times in a month. Before the end of the first month, everyone knows team goals, who we are, and we know one another; as opposed to a team that meets once a month. So moving to another stage will depend on the frequency of the meetings.

Now, **storming stage.** Here, opinions on members are being formed and may be shared. We have done all the icebreakers possible. We know what we are doing and everything, now we can see a team member and say, "hmm, this person looks like somebody that would be proud," or "that one looks like somebody that is just cocky or maybe snobbish." Then you have people that are not snobbish or people that think that other people are snobbish and are separating themselves from the people that are "snobbish." The leader emphasizes tolerance. Cliques emerge in the storming stage, and then teams now question their leader. Does this person even know what they are talking about, can they even lead us, why were they made our leader? That is the storming stage.

Then the **norming stage** is like normalizing. Issues are resolved, members trust each other, and everything is now kind of coming back to normal as the team has now accepted itself. They have set the goals that they have come together to achieve, criticisms are held back, and conflict is avoided. No one wants to step on anyone's toes, maybe because we have misjudged people and situations in the two earlier stages and we have realized our misjudgments. So everyone is being at their best with mutual respect. No one wants to fight anymore. We are now trying to focus on the goal – personal, team, and teammate goals at this stage; teams now band together against other teams. For example, a team works out of a room where they have their resources; paper, copier, etc., and someone outside the team comes into their room to use their resources. Everyone will be like, "No, don't come here and use up our resources." So in that situation, everything is normal. The team is normal, and they are now working together against other forces outside their team. The norming stage lasts as long as established goals are being worked on and the frequency of team meetings

Finally, the **performing stage** is when roles within the team are established. Everyone knows their task and assignment. There is synergy within the team, and everyone is working together. Goals are achieved faster together, members can use their discretion to do something, and when they come together, they can update the team and be like, "I handled this situation when I saw that it was a problem, and no one would have a problem with that" – no micromanaging. Arguments should be allowed, and the team jointly decides how to handle them.

The "silent" stage of team development is the **adjourning stage,** where the team has achieved most of the goals they set and there is less workload. Finishing touches are being put in the work, and the members are documenting details of their tasks and achievements. Therefore, the team disperses. It is important to know that as soon as something changes within a team, the team resets and goes back to the forming stage. For example, if a new member is added to the team, they will go through the "we don't know you yet" phase, trying to size up the new member. Or if the team leader changes, the team will reset again. Those are the stages of forming a team.

Conflict in a Team
There are different kinds of conflicts in teams. **Cognitive conflicts, which are called C-type conflicts,** and are based on a difference of opinion and expertise. Members of the team conflict because they have different experiences based on different capacities they have occupied in the past or that they occupy. Two different people, two different types of expertise and experience. And they just conflict based on that.

Affective conflicts or A-type conflicts are caused by emotional reactions to a disagreement. Two people may not agree on a process, but then they make it personal. They fight the person instead of working to agree on the process.

Role ambiguity is another type of conflict in a team. It is a situation where no one knows exactly what role they are to occupy or what tasks they are to accomplish. No one has been assigned any task, but everyone wants to do what is easiest. "I will do this one and will leave the rest. I don't care if anybody does the rest or not; I will just pretend that I cannot see what is going on." There are no clearly defined roles.

Role conflicts - an employee does not know what role they should play. There are too many demands and employees are pulled in different directions. Role conflict is further broken down into:

1. **Inter-role conflict** is when an employee is split between which roles they should play. For example, this COVID lockdown period, where parents are expected to homeschool their kids. Because they cannot go to daycare or school, and they also have their day jobs, which role do they play in the eight to nine hours they have during the day? Or like a doctor that has a personal family emergency and still gets called into the hospital because a patient needs them urgently, which role will they perform in such a situation? That is inter-role conflict.

2. **Inter-sender conflict** is a situation where management expects one thing from the team leader; "this is how you should push the employees to deliver results, this is what we expect," but the employees on the other hand do not have the tools that they need. So, the employees are sending the team leader to the management with their requests, but management is not having it and still expecting the team leader to get the maximum results from the employees. Two different expectations from the two groups of people. It is a situation where someone is caught between opposing expectations.

3. **Intra-sender conflict** when someone that is in charge of enforcing the rule is the one pushing an employee to break the rule. That is intra-sender conflict. For example, a compliance person in a bank who knows that staff cannot provide banking information to a third party without the

express instruction of the account holder encourages the bank staff to break the rules. That is intra-sender conflict.

4. **Intra-role conflict** is when an employee is being asked to do activities that go against their ethics.

Status conflict is the disagreement about someone's status in a team, like earlier when we talked about questioning the leadership of a team in the storming stage of team formation. Team members are debating what qualification this person has to be their leader, or questioning if the leader even deserves their respect. Status conflict can be directed at the team leader; it can be to any member of the team. It is like sizing people up to determine what level of respect they deserve if any.

Social loafing is when a team member is not pulling their weight or doing their part to ensure the team meets its goals in a teamwork situation; but maybe when they work by themselves, they will possibly do better on their own.

Identifying Team Dynamics

We can know the dynamics in a team-based on:

1. **The communication channels** - that they choose to use; overt or covert.

Overt communication channels are tools that are designed for communication, emails, phone calls, chats, like intra-organization chat applications, tools that are designed for communication.

Covert communication channels are not designed for communication; those are not the channels that have been agreed on to pass across important information. It can just be pre-agreed between team members. "When I do this, just know that this is what I mean." You can know what dynamics exist in a team by examining their communication channels.

2. **Functional roles** - are they task-related or about maintaining the activities in the group? i.e. Are they all about being focused on what they need to do, the decision, and the actions, or are they about being friendly with each other, building a sense of identity, and developing social relationships? There is a need to balance the functional roles in a team for effective group operations.

3. **Problem-solving and Decision making** - How does the team solve its problems? How do they make their decisions?

Ignored suggestions. Are suggestions sometimes ignored? Some people's suggestions may be ignored.

Minority rule is when less than 50% of the group make a decision just because they are loud, pushy, popular, or they are the elite in the group – the minority just decides. *The majority rule* is when more than 50% agree on a decision. That is another way to know what team dynamics the team is operating.

Consensus. A consensus is when every member of the team supports an idea. No one is forcing anything on anyone, no one is shutting anyone down, but after a while, each member supports whatever decision they are making over time. So that is another type of team dynamics.

4. **Group norms** - what are the agreed behaviors of the group? It can be positive or negative. For example, if we are working towards the same goal, we are actively engaged and we have agreed that this is how we are going to conduct ourselves. Then if a group is actively disengaged, all of them will be acting in a way that harms the organization. They may encourage or aid each other to not do any productive work until a manager comes to inspect.

5. **Leadership and Authority** - are they focused on actively sharing responsibilities and being accountable? It

can result in a kind of team dynamics. Is leadership steering the team towards synergy?

6. **Synergistic team characteristics** - Synergy is when a team is working efficiently together. They support each other, they listen to each other, clarify issues that they do not understand, and they comfort each other in their disagreement – they do not engage in an affective conflict where conflicts are made personal; they just deal with whatever issue is on the ground. There is a consensus in decision making, and teams accept each other, leading to quality of performance.

Everything just goes smoothly, and they deal with matters civilly.

Team Interventions

Intervention is when there is a need to start or stop a behavior. The first time I heard of intervention was in a movie, where intervention was being staged for someone that was being wayward and they needed that person to behave properly or to change their ways. That is what intervention is, stopping or starting an action. It is an intentional action to improve a team. Now, as it pertains to a team, getting the team to stop an action or to start an action, that is team intervention. There are two main ways for team interventions to be done; either by **process consultation and team building** or by **third-party interventions.**

Process consultation and team building - team building is a way of getting rid of personal barriers and improving trust within a team. Process consultation and team building have three different levels:

A. Individual intervention, intervening with each team member, one on one. That is done by conducting *interviews,* getting everyone to change their mind or change their mindset. Individual interventions are also done by ***360degree feedback,*** which is interviewing the team members, peers, managers, customers, subordinates, or suppliers - interviewing everyone that matters to a team member's performance or work. The next level in process consultation is;

B. Group interventions, mean a group changing together and fast. It is initiated by the team, and the team assigns roles to each member. It can be done with the aid of a ***team checklist,*** where the group checks off behavior changes or development as they happen; this is what we expect, these are the behaviors we want to start or stop, are they happening yet? You check them as you go along as a group. Group interventions can also be done using ***team surveys,*** which help to understand the team's thoughts or needs or what needs to go. You survey the team to know, what are we thinking as a group? What do we need to stop? What do we need to start? What needs to go? Also, group interventions can be done by ***facilitated goal setting*** - where you get a facilitator to help the team to get a clear picture of where they want to go. ***Problem-solving*** - defining the problem, you know the different stages of problem-solving up until the point when they standardize and accept the solution that they end up with. SWOT analysis - defining the strengths, weaknesses, opportunities, and threats of a team, and then getting that facilitator to bring everything together. Facilitated goal setting involves a third party which is the facilitator that would guide the team or the group in changing the behaviors that they want to stop or starting the behaviors that they want to start.

C. Intervening for integrating groups with the rest of the organization. We assume that the teams, in this case, are doing different things that are not aligned with organizational goals. And an alignment is needed, that is the third part of the process consultation intervention. There is a need to intervene to integrate the group or groups with the rest of the organization. One way to do that is by strategic planning, aligning the groups with the organization's strategy – vision, mission, goals, and objectives, and specializing in the overall plan. So each team knows their part in the picture. We know where each team fits into this organizational strategy as a whole. Also, stakeholder mapping, aligning the powers and interests of all stakeholders, and knowing who to update when things change. Stakeholder mapping involves knowing which stakeholder has high power and high interest, high power and low interest, low power and low interest, and low power but high interest. When someone has high power and high interest, that person has to be kept updated. Stakeholder mapping is essentially knowing who matters to what extent. Someone that has low interest and low power does not have the power to change or do anything about the organization's direction, and they do not have to be updated as often. Third-party intervention as a means of team intervention. When a team cannot solve its problem by itself, then they involve a mediator to resolve that conflict for them, and in that process, they express the team's unmet needs. The mediator tries to find a compromise for each member of the team. Research shows that in 80% of all conflicts, it is possible to find a win-win by accommodating each team member; compromising, and collaborating.

Team Members Competencies and Capabilities
To know the capabilities of team members, there is a need to **examine what is required.** What was the plan? What did we set out to do? Can they do the tasks that were planned?

Are they capable of doing what we have planned to do? Do they have the level of skills, competencies, and experience needed to do what the team has set out to do?

Next is to **evaluate what is available,** what do we currently have? – Examining the current state. That is, evaluating the current performance to determine what we have, and then doing development plans. Once you have done a performance evaluation, and things are not where they are supposed to be, there is a gap, then you carry out a development plan. Also, you can know the development plans in that instance by examining the current state; what plan we set out for development in the first place, and also knowing what skills the team has. So in this team, depending on what they are meant to do, for example, a construction team, do we have someone that has experience in chopping down big obstructing trees and creating furniture from it for this house that we are constructing? Do we have people that have those kinds of skills, those kinds of experiences? So that is how you can judge whether a team member can function properly in the team they have been assigned. The last step is to **determine the gaps and take action.** In the second step, you are assessing what the current stage is. So you have already known what the plan is, and where we are currently; now merge it. Is there a disconnect? Measure your plan against your current state and then identify the gaps. What should stay? What should go? What should we stop doing? What should we continue doing or what should we now bring in? What skills do we need that we do not currently have? What is acceptable and what is not acceptable? Is it acceptable to have new joiners, maybe entry-level people take charge of major projects in an organization? Would you put all of them in a team, is that acceptable? Or would you need to bring in other people that have more experience or varying sets of skills? That is how you can assess team member competencies, and what they are capable of, and then make changes that are needed.

Employee Engagement

What is employee engagement? Essentially it is when employees are engaged with the organization. It means to be involved in, to be enthusiastic about, and to be committed to the workplace. It's when employees are involved in what is going on in the organization and are enthusiastic about what is going on. They're committed to the workplace. So in an organizational climate that is not aligned with the culture that management had in mind - a vision of the ideal way in which they believe things are being done; wanting employees to be the best, and giving them the best tools so that they can give their best, assuming that is ideally what management has in mind; if that is not aligned with the climate - what is going on - then employees cannot be said to be engaged. Employees need to be actively involved in what's going on in an organization. They need to be enthusiastic about it, and they need to have an emotional commitment to the organization. Then and only then can we say employees are engaged. Employee engagement leads to discretionary effort, which means going the extra mile. When an employee is sold out to the organization, they are going the extra mile without complaining; they're giving their best. They are like Star employees, and that means they are fully engaged. Engagement also leads to the overall wellbeing and profitability of the organization. So when everybody is a star employee, everyone is doing their share. Whatever kind of business that the organization is involved in, everyone is giving their best, which in turn, translates to everyone's wellbeing and mental state. The climate is not hostile; everybody is happy. This translates to profitability for the organization, and if it is a publicly traded company, you can see it in the stock market i.e. how the stocks are performing as well.

Employee engagement is very important because it has so many repercussions if there is a lack of engagement. Also, employee engagement is vital to managing people, for leadership to be able to manage the employees. Employee engagement is vital because if the employees are not engaged, it is like management is saying one thing and the employees are somewhere else physically and mentally. Sometimes surveys can be done to gain insight into how much employees are engaged, same as understanding an organization's climate - to get employees' feedback; more like taking the organization's pulse through surveys. Leaders need to improve employee engagement to achieve efficient delivery by employees; to ensure that employees are delivering their tasks fully, going the extra mile, and giving the discretionary effort. Employee engagement predicts employee satisfaction. When employees are engaged, giving their best, enthusiastic, and committed to the organization, then you know that they are satisfied. Now, a simple equation for this is motivation + satisfaction + commitment to the organization is what leads to the discretionary effort, which is the extra mile that employees are giving.

History of Employee Engagement : Scientific Management

Employee engagement has been a concept from the time of management theories, from the 1800s, where we had scientific management theory, employee motivation, and satisfaction theory; and now we have employee engagement. So, employee engagement has always been featured in management theories. The earliest management theory is the scientific management theory, which Frederick Taylor is said to be the father of. The theory believes in effectively using business resources, which also includes human resources.

The theory states that it is important to scientifically study the motives of employees. It was created to increase productivity through engagement, harmony, and combined intellectual activities. An environment where human efforts have to be maximized, so I am thinking like a factory where they want employees to deliver to the maximum. Maybe they may not even have time to use the washroom.

Employees have to be fully driven to produce results through engagement. This approach emphasizes employees' interest in doing their job to improve their skills, so it rewards aligning beliefs. It believes that rewarding employees with aligned beliefs leads to motivation and increases employees' desire to continually improve. Also, employees need to understand what the expectations are, for them to be judged fairly - performance management somehow features here. Employees need to know what the targets are, for them to be fairly judged, and for there to be a reward for good performance. That's basically what scientific management is all about.

It is aimed at increasing productivity through engagement. When employees are fully engaged, have satisfaction on the job, and they're committed to the job, then scientific management believes that there will be productivity. It also emphasizes an employee's interest in their job. If a floor worker gets promoted and recognized, then they want to do more. For example, if they want to be a floor manager, whatever it takes to be floor manager they are interested in doing it. It motivates employees, and the desire to want to be better, to do more. Employees need feedback, which lets employees understand expectations.

History of Employee Engagement: Motivation & Satisfaction

The next stage after the idea that employees must be fully maximized is motivation and satisfaction. This part of employee engagement history is the theory of motivation. I am sure you are familiar with this theory.

The first is **Maslow's Hierarchy of Needs.** It says that employee motivation depends on which needs have been met. It has five hierarchies divided into *basic needs (physiological), social (psychological), and self-actualization needs (fulfillment).* Basic needs are food, clothing, and shelter. When employees are fed, they want their next needs met. When people are hungry, they hardly want to be social. "I don't want to play with anyone if I am hungry. I don't even care about my self-esteem if I am hungry." So the needs that are met lead to the needs that are yet to be met. That's what motivates. When I am fed, my next motivation depends on what other needs I want to meet. Basic needs are physiological needs like water, food, warmth, rest, and security/safety. Do I have a job? Am I just an employee that will just show up? And if there is a need for me, I will be able to work on that day, or do I have a place within the organization? That is basic needs.

Psychological needs are belongingness and esteem; friendship. When employees have satisfied their basic needs, they want to then go on to the next need. So what would motivate such an employee that already has a job and is fed? Do I have meaningful interactions at work? Do I have friends in the organization? Am I valued?

For self-actualization needs, people that have met the four previous needs (Physiological, Safety, Social, Esteem) are now looking for self-actualization, to be all they can be, and actualize as many dreams as possible. That is the link between employee engagement and what motivates employees. The second is the **ERG theory**. It is the same thing as Maslow's theory, but instead of saying that the needs are grouped into basic, social, and actualization, they are grouped into existence needs, relatedness needs, and growth needs (Maslow's first two needs are physiological and safety needs), which translate to existence needs. Do I feel like I am not at the bottom of the food chain? Do I have a home to lay my head to rest? food, warmth, a place to call work where I get money to feed myself and meet other needs? Next is relatedness needs, which is the same thing as social needs. You want to make friends, and you want to feel valued. Last is growth needs, which is the same thing as self-actualization needs, and the final one in Maslow's hierarchy of needs. Next is the **two-factor theory,** which says there are motivators, and there are hygiene factors. Motivators depend on what the employees need. So if you give employees something that they do not need, they are not motivated, but if you give them what they need, they are motivated. Then hygiene needs are just the minimum. If they are there, fine, but it will not motivate employees, and if they are not there, then they will cause dissatisfaction for the employee. If you give an employee a nice office, fine, it may not necessarily motivate them, but if they are in an office with dilapidated furniture for example, then definitely, that would frustrate. The two factor theory; motivators, things that motivate employees; and hygiene, which does not necessarily motivate, but if they are not there, then employees are dissatisfied.

Needs theory is next. It says that employees have only three needs. The need for achievement, affiliation, and power. And that is what motivates them.

Then **Expectancy theory** talks about employees choosing to behave in a certain way if they expect that they will be rewarded for it - employees expect that their efforts will lead to the possibility of getting something in return. Now, instrumentality means a reward following whatever effort employees put in. And then valence asks what value does the reward carry? For example, maybe there is an Instagram, challenge, or promotion, and the designated reward is a subscription to a service you do not use or plan to use. Do you need it? No. Do you value it? Not necessarily. So that will not be a motivating factor. That explains expectancy theory. Employees will be motivated by the fact that the effort they put into a competition will yield a reward and they value that reward.

Equity theory says motivation depends on the feeling of fairness. If employees feel like they are being treated fairly, then they will be motivated. You can also link that back to an organization's climate because it is about perception. If I perceive that management only favors a certain group of people, then I am not motivated to give them my best because I perceive them as not being fair anyway; so it does not matter what I do.

The goal-setting theory states that with the right goals, motivation and productivity can be increased. So, let me go into that further. Once you set the right goal, employees would be motivated. I believe this places employee motivation or engagement solely on management, depending on how the goals are set or how the organization's strategy is put together - top to bottom/bottom to top approach. If the right goals are set, the goals are clear, they are challenging enough for the employees, employees get feedback, and if employees' tasks are challenging enough but not too tough, then employees will be motivated. That is what goal-setting theory talks about.

Finally, in the history of motivation and satisfaction is the **job characteristics model,** which says motivation depends on what a job contains; what kind of job am I doing? Is it just for an employee to stand at a spot and when there is a task for them, you call on them? People will not be motivated to do those kinds of jobs. Motivation depends on what kind of job people do.

Employee Engagement: Since the 1990s

The concept of employee engagement came about in the 1990s. We said employee engagement involves commitment, satisfaction, and motivation. So we have seen theories of motivation, and how it can lead to satisfaction and commitment. In this concept, there is a chance for employees to be engaged, and there is a chance for employees to be disengaged. So it is not just about engagement since the 1990s. Employees can either be engaged or not, and the difference is, does the organization allow employees' personality and creativity to shine through? This can lead to employee engagement. Employees feel like they are valued when they can bring up suggestions, when they are not shut down, regardless of the suggestions being implemented or not. They can then give their commitment to the organization, as they are motivated and satisfied. And if suggestions are not allowed, like in an instance when employees try to bring up an idea and they are faced with an attitude almost saying, "What are you talking about?" then employees can be disengaged. That is the difference between the two. And when employees are disengaged, they just do what they are told like robots. No one wants their ideas, maybe they know how to do something better, or not. Disengagement threatens organizations' survival. That is very key, because if all employees are disengaged, then they are not giving their best, and the organization is not achieving its goals. It affects organizational output, how employees relate to all the stakeholders including customers, and it affects profitability. The concept of employee engagement is still developing because it only began in the 1990s. Some schools of thought even now talk about organizational fitness, just like in a gym to human fitness. I believe that as the thought develops, we will hear more about it in publications.

Models of Employee Engagement
There are models of employee engagement, and some people and organizations have come up with these models.

Gallop Model
This model uses a 12-question survey and is based on employee performance and development needs. Each element of the Gallop model, that is, each question asked in the Gallop model, is linked to key organizational outcomes and best predicts employee and workgroup performance. They ask 12 questions that can predict performance. Gallop says that employees can either be engaged, not engaged, or actively disengaged. We know what employee engagement means - employees are motivated, they are satisfied, they are committed, and are giving their best. Those that are not engaged, those factors (motivation, satisfaction, commitment, and going the extra mile) are not present. Now you also have people that are actively disengaged, not only are they not engaged, but they are acting on their disengagement. The fact that they are disengaged is making them act it out. An example of someone that is disengaged is

a customer service person shouting at everyone on the phone, or at anyone that walks into the office. Someone not giving the best service; that person is actively trying to sabotage the company. That is what Gallop's Q12 model says. This model then goes further to examine levels of engagement or disengagement by investigating **Basic needs;** what role is given to the employee? What can the employee give back? Do they have the right tools? Do employees know what is expected of them? So before we blame that customer service person, are the phone lines working very well? Or maybe whenever they answer the phone, they receive prank or scam calls. And then the next time the line goes through, still frustrated by the bad line, they act up and it is a customer calling! - Do employees have what they need, are the tools working? And do they know what is expected of them and what they can give back? The Gallop Q12 model also investigates *Management support;* do employees feel like they are being supported by management? For example, if they have a need, can they speak up? Everyone is human; if something comes up at home, can they speak up? Do they feel supported or is the leadership just interested in what they can get from the employees? Like "keep your home responsibilities away from work," etc.? Do employees feel supported by management? Is there an opportunity for them to do their best? Can an employee say, "I want to take half of the day off, because I have to attend to my child," or "can I complete my hours at home?" Do employees feel supported enough to ask for that? Because it is all about doing the job, not necessarily about the location, as COVID-19 has taught us. Is there room for that? Also, are the employees being commended or complimented for their performances or contributions? How often are these comments or compliments given? Does anyone care about me as a person in the organization? Does anybody care about my growth? Or do they just want to leave me in the photocopy room forever? Nobody cares if I have done extra classes. If I am interested in any other position in the organization, nobody is even asking about it. This can lead to engagement or disengagement, and that is on the management support level. ***Teamwork*** is also investigated under Gallop's Q12 model. Do employees feel like they are connected to the work? Are they connected to the organization? That would also determine if they are engaged or not or actively engaged, according to Gallop. When investigating teamwork, ask questions like, do employees feel like their opinion counts? Do employees feel like their organization is doing work that matters? For example, there are some organizations that we have now, I am not sure if they should be called organizations or setups, that recruit people to make scam calls; they have employees too, right? They have a leadership team. They have all those things. Do such employees feel like their organization is doing work that matters? Positive work? Do they feel like they are alone in the work that they are doing? Does their hard work matter? Do they have a social system in the office? Do they have a support network? Do I have people around me that make the day worthwhile, when we do take a break from work? Because no one is doing eight hours straight of work. You need to take that break and bounce off someone else to renew your energy. Is that available to me in an organization?

Lastly, Gallop's Q12 Model investigates ***Growth*** i.e. is there an opportunity for employees to learn to grow in the organization? Can they succeed together with the people in their organization? Are they headed in the same direction? Can they innovate together? That is engagement. Gallop's model investigates these issues at different levels. Each of the levels preceding growth can happen in any order, but employees cannot get to the stage of engagement where employees are interested in learning, growing, and innovating, without the basic needs addressed, without management support present, and without teamwork present. The levels can be simultaneous, but level four is only achievable by having gone through the other levels or the presence of the other three levels.

Only engaged employees can think of the organization as a collective and be interested in its overall success because they have personalized the workplace.

And one more thing I want to mention about this Gallop model and actively disengaged employees. You can think of the organization as a ship. Some people are engaged in making sure that things are working. Some people are just there; they are not bothered about what is going on; they are neither engaged nor disengaged. And some are actively disengaged, and as such are very dangerous to everyone on board because they are the ones actively reversing the positive efforts of the engaged people, and putting all their efforts into ensuring that the ship sinks. So that is why it is important to be able to know what level employees are at and be able to know what to do about them. If there are actively disengaged people in an organization, they can ruin everything that everyone else is doing.

Eon Hewitt Model and Towers Watson Model

These two organizations use software measurement to determine employee engagement. The software is used to create surveys that ask employees a series of questions, about 50 to 100 each time, whichever way the surveys are structured to measure employee engagement.

Drivers of Employee Engagement

What drives employee engagement? What makes employees interested in being engaged? Employees are interested in engagement when there is **clarity of expectations,** employees know what is expected of them; and **task significance,** their tasks, their work makes sense, and they are making progress. **Self-efficacy** is when they feel selfsufficient and confident in their capabilities to make some decisions. I do not need anyone to tell me what to do every time. When those are present, those *motivate* employees.

Then **autonomy of ideas** and opinions, along with **effective feedback,** drives *satisfaction,* meaning I can think of how to do certain tasks, even though I have a checklist of how to do them or a process of what to do. But as long as I meet the goal and I do not get scolded for it, then I am satisfied with my work.

Effective feedback - am I getting feedback? Do I know why I have been scored as such in my performance appraisal? Do I know why my promotion is being delayed, or do I just have to wait another six months? Or I do not know because I am in a don't ask, don't tell environment?

Also, when employees have **rewarding relationships** within the organization, when they find the **values of the organization and the leadership team** challenging to them like there is something worth admiring about the organization and its leadership, and when there are **opportunities to grow,** then employees are *committed* to that organization. Drivers of engagement are factors that lead to motivation, satisfaction, and commitment. And all of these drivers are good for all stakeholders i.e. Customers, partners, employees. Therefore, *HR programs should focus on leadership's buy-in of employee engagement and thoughtful* *communication.* If there is anything worth saying to the employees, is it communicated sensitively? Not just "we don't care how you feel or what your feelings are, we are just going to say anything we want, whenever." *HR programs should focus on rewarding relationships* and ensure that they are supported by the organizations' structure. *The employees feel empowered* and the *process is carefully designed* such that there is two-way respect between the organization and employees - everybody feels valued and the *employees are involved.*

Change Management

What are we changing? Through the course of this content, we have identified several points of inefficiencies that need addressing for any organization's effectiveness. I imagine everything cannot be 100% wrong in an organization, neither can everything be 100% right. When that is understood, HRPs are expected to keep their eyes out for opportunities to change positively and help guide their organizations towards efficiency. Since we know the common saying that change is the only constant thing, therefore organizations must adapt or go extinct.

I have an example here of Debenhams and Boohoo.

Debenhams is a department store that is about 208 years old, while Boohoo is just 15 years old. And recently, Boohoo acquired Debenhams. Debenhams is going out of business, being acquired by a 15-year-old company. This raised curiosity as to what could have happened. According to an article by BBC News, Debenhams refused to improve or change what they were offering to customers. They left things as they were. Boohoo is an online company. Though Debenhams also went online, their product offering was still lacking, which did not make much of Debenhams' online presence. The article also stated some financial problems. They doubled the number of physical stores that they had and had leases going up to 35 years, which increased by 2.5% annually. Debenhams kind of shot themselves in the leg that way instead of adapting to market trends. Had they done that, they probably would still be existing today and not acquired by another organization.

What is change? – It is aligning or mobilizing employees when there is a need to change to deliver expected outcomes. Say Debenhams wanted to change, but they did not align the employees in such a way that they would be interested in the change, they would still have had a problem. Now, because change is inevitable, it is important to be able to align and mobilize employees to change when there is a need for a change and update employees on what the change would mean in an organization.

Reactions to Change
Now that we know that there is no dodging change, we need to understand how people react to change. The first reaction is *denial,* where employees in the context of an organization think the change is not possible. This happens when the delivery of the change information is faulty, like when the information about the said change comes from the grapevine - we will know more about this when we discuss communication. Next to denial is *resistance,* when employees see that change is inevitable, they start resisting it, and then *exploration* starts as the change is happening because employees now know they cannot stop the change. They start considering the change by "dipping one foot in the pond." The last stage in reactions to change is *acceptance.* At this stage, employees have determined to make the change succeed. People resist change because they see the change as a threat to their interests. They do not want to fix what they believe is not broken, and they fear they would not adapt easily. They do not trust the change. They have opposing views as to the need for a change, what to change, and how to go about changing. This could be because they are just too used to the current state of things.

How to Lead Change Management: Lewin's Model
There are different models to leading change management, starting with Lewin's model. Think of ice blocks. Say you

want to change the shape or appearance of ice blocks, from little squares into maybe little star shapes. You have to **unfreeze** it, pour the water in the new form in the new mold (The **change** activity) that you want, and then **refreeze** it. That is what the Lewin model is saying here. It also states that there are two forces in play for any change activity. There are forces for the change and forces against the change. Now, the job of the change manager, which in this case would be the HRPs, is to address the forces that are against the change; those are the ones to focus on. "This is why we need to change, this is what change would mean." If you give attention to the reasons why the change is needed, then people would resist further. They will find excuses as to why those reasons for change are invalid. Once it is clear that there is a need for change, focus on the forces that are against the change and address those.

How to Lead Change Management: Kotter's 8 Steps
Under Kotter's model, there are eight steps to follow to see the change activity through.

Step 1 is to **create a sense of urgency**, the manager or the leader creates a compelling case as to why there is a need to change and inspire employees to move. The role of the manager or the leader in an organization cannot be overemphasized. We saw this when we discussed the four basic culture types. A leader cannot just be "I am only meant to be seen, I don't get my hands dirty with work," or "I am just this mystery far away," because they have a lot of work to do in managing change.

Step 2 is to **create guiding coalitions,** have change champions within the organization. Get some employees that will be interested and willing to help drive the change. Step 3 is to **develop the vision and strategy,** which has to be short, clear, and understandable. Create an emotional element within the change such as "the reason why we have to change is so that we do not go out of business; so that loads of families that have worked in the same organization from generation to generation can continue to do so." Step 4 is to **communicate the vision and the strategy** - the chosen communication channel is going to matter when leading change management according to Kotter's model. Step 5 is **to empower broad-based action.** The change manager needs to listen to the employees that will be affected by the change, help them overcome their fears and any objections to the change, and create a feedback loop for employees to come back, in case they still have any problems with understanding why there is need for the change. Step 6 is to **generate short-term wins** - show benefits early – "this is what we are trying to do and this is what the benefits are"; show it early. That is like agile development, where you show incremental benefits of whatever new thing you are trying to do. Maybe you are trying to build a customer service system and automate the process, and the customer service person believes they would be out of a job as a result. There will be the need to show them early that they will not be out of their job. Explain how the system is going to make them do their job better. Give them that solution early on in the chain so that they can see that change is not the enemy. Repeat steps 1 to 6 as often as possible, to maintain the momentum.

This brings us to Step 7, which is to **consolidate gains and produce more change,** i.e. build on the momentum of the change. Now that everyone is on board, they know the benefits of the change; do not just leave it there.

Lastly, step 8 is to **anchor the change in the culture of the organization** because we said culture is what is taught from existing employees to new employees, what they believe, what they value, what they show; a physical manifestation of the culture. So that way, the new culture or the change sticks. Since we are changing culture, culture is ideally the way things should be done and how things are done. That is what change is about, to ensure that the change sticks and is embedded in the culture of the organization.

How to Lead Change Management: The Action Research Model
This model seeks to improve professional practice by enabling double-loop learning. Double-loop learning is going back to double-check a solution, to measure the solution you think you have, to see if it covers all bases. So action research model involves **identifying the problem, consulting the experts** to solve the problem, **gathering the needed data,** giving **feedback to the client,** doing a **joint diagnosis,** followed by **joint action planning,** and finally **taking action.** The double-loop learning in this model is to gather data again after taking action and feeding that back to the client. Rechecking solutions to ensure everything is as it should be.

How to Lead Change Management: Positive Change Model
The positive change model focuses on what is going well, not even thinking about any negatives, and creates a positive expectation that will direct behavior towards new beliefs. So we are not focusing on what is wrong, we are focusing on what the organization is doing well, and we want to continue that. Even though we want to change, we are focusing on how our current practices go smoothly with our new beliefs.

The positive change model also enables double-loop learning. It **identifies the focus of the change, finds out how best to carry out the change, and discovers key themes** - what is standing out? i.e. what is obvious? what stands out for us? - then **identify the future that you want** - envision the kind of future that you want - then design ways to create the future i.e. **take action**. The double-loop learning in this model is done after you take action in step 5 to go back to step 2, which is to engage appreciative inquiry i.e. finding out the best practices. To ensure that the actions align with best practices, does it work with the future we want to create?

Organizational Learning
There are two types of organizational learning, we mentioned one of them before. One is the process of single loop learning and the second one is double-loop learning.

Organizational learning is the process of detecting and correcting errors in an organization. Trying to find errors and trying to correct them in an organization - we are trying to learn.

In single-loop learning, it focuses on following rules and operating norms. For example, I know that if I flick the light switch, the room would light up. It is about taking action and getting results. Simple, straightforward, single-loop learning.

Double-loop learning is critically questioning the rules. If I flick on this switch, what if the light comes on or what if it does not? What if the light is dim? You question the basic rules, think outside the box, and are creative to figure out what is the best approach to do things. So if the light does not come on, what do I do?

Question = get results
Question assumptions and beliefs = Take action = get results

Question what you think you know; question the rules. What seems cast in stone? Would it work in this situation? Is it the only way to do this? So that is two types of organizational learning.

Change Management Tools
We have the critical path, PERT chart, and Gantt chart. **The critical path** is the longest route for a project to be completed. It charts the relationship between planned activities and the time it takes to complete them. It shows all activities, which if delayed, can delay the project completion. So with the critical path, say we want to do this project, how long will it take us to do the project? Which one is the longest route? We have different alternatives A, B, and C? If we choose alternative A, how long does it take? How long does B take? How long does C take? Then choose the longest route as it has no slack time.

PERT chart also uses an overlapping approach just like the critical path. It uses three-point estimates for the duration of the project, and it does not assume that project durations are known 100%. So instead of saying alternative A, B, C, it has the optimistic - it will take us 3 days to finish this project. The pessimistic: it can be up to 8 days, most likely 6 days. So optimistically, we are going to finish the project in 3 weeks. Pessimistically maybe 8 weeks, most likely, 6 weeks.

The Gantt chart depicts each task that has to be complete, against how long it takes to complete each task. It is used for projects with lower complexity. Say we want to build a house, we know the foundation is first. The Gantt chart would say the foundation would take maybe two weeks to complete. While the foundation is being set, is there something else that can start, or is there something we can do before we start the foundation? Or after the foundation, when can the next project start? It lists all the tasks that need to be done, shows the time factor for each activity, shows which one should start before the other, and which one has to end before another one starts. It depicts each milestone with a diamond shape. The Gantt chart simply articulates and communicates a project in a diagrammatic form. It shows you we want to pour the foundation. This is when we start, this is how much time we have. Each bar on the chart is as wide as the time allotted to the activity it represents. For example one week = one bar; 2 weeks = two bars, etc.

Communicating a Change Activity
We said one of the ways to lead a change activity is by communicating effectively. That makes it important to look at the communication process. **The process of communication** is that the sender thinks of what he wants to say and decides how he wants to say it; that is encoding, choosing the communication channel, and then transmitting to the receiver. Then the receiver perceives the information and determines what the message means, thereby decoding it and understanding it; that is the communication process. The sender on one hand and receiver on the other encoding and decoding the message passed between both of them respectively. This process is said to be incomplete without feedback so that the sender knows that what was communicated to the receiver is understood. That is a complete communication process.

Now, how do we communicate change? What **communication path** do we use? *Downward* *communication* is directed to the employees from the top. *Upward communication* is directed from employees to the management. *Horizontal communication* is between peers, say maybe two managers on the same level passing information to one another. *Formal communication* is using designated paths of communication, like we said, emails, phone calls, internal chat, etc. *Informal communication* is communication channels that have not been designated for use when passing official information. *Grapevine* is truthful communication that has not yet been communicated formally. Remember that we said one of the reactions to change is denial, and that is when that change is communicated through the grapevine. So, employees know that this change is coming, but it is yet to be communicated officially. *Intentional communication* is deliberate information meant to be shared or passed across.

Unintentional communication is letting out a secret without premeditation, without a prior plan. For example, when a clique within a team is communicating with signals etc., not knowing that the rest of the team understands their supposedly secret communication.

Non-verbal communication is communicating but not with words. It may be a kind of unintentional communication. The example that comes to mind is the TikTok challenge that happened in the year 2020, when people pretending to be social media brand influencers, tried to catch the reaction of their relatives on camera to untrue exaggerated pranks they were playing. The person whose reaction they were trying to catch on camera knew their statements were untrue; however, they were unaware of the prank and their reactions were golden! That is an example of nonverbal communication.

Interferences to Communication

If communication can contribute to an organization's effectiveness, why then are there still challenges? We will be examining some barriers to effective communication. When communicating, it is important to ensure that the language in use can be understood by the receiver and that the receiver understands. You cannot be speaking Dutch to an English speaker who is not bilingual in both languages; that is one of the interferences to communication - **language differences.** The next one is **cultural differences**. Culture is how someone shows their perception of things, so it is important to ensure that with the culture, you find a common ground between the sender and receiver's culture. Otherwise, that difference can be a hindrance to communication. **Gender differences** - these days we have to be sensitive to what we say to people generally, and especially to people of a different gender to us. You cannot make insensitive comments around those of a different gender, as that can be misunderstood or misperceived just because of how you have chosen to communicate. Some manner of speaking that would fly with men, which they sometimes call locker room talk, would not necessarily sit well with women. Think around communication barriers based on gender. Next is the **frame of reference,** which is an offshoot of experiences. The sender's frame of reference is based on their experience, which is what they would reference while communicating with someone else. This could lead to the sender giving examples about something the receiver does not know anything about and the sender's meaning is lost in that communication. Someone who does not share the same experience or exposure to the same things the speaker is referencing may be lost in such a conversation, which means communication has not happened and no message has been passed along. The next barrier to communication is **jargon,** maybe medical jargon. Each profession has its register of languages and choice of words, which means a different thing to someone outside that profession. This may lead to a complete misunderstanding. If the receiver is not a doctor or a medical person, and the sender is using terms that only people in that profession would understand, it may be acronyms, slangs, etc., the receiver definitely will not understand what the sender is saying or take it to mean something else entirely, which is a barrier to communication. Then the **mum effect** is just like what it sounds. When you ask someone to give their opinion, and they do not use words and they go like "mmm mm mmm," not wanting to say the truth about how they feel or what they think because the person responsible for what they have been asked to give their opinion about is present. For example, if a friend who has been boasting about their partner's cooking invites you to their home for dinner, and you are meant to rate the cooking. The meal you just experienced is not as great, but because the cook is present, you either say it is good or you just keep quiet, or you nod, hiding under the guise of the wine in your mouth because you do not want to give negative feedback with the cook present. In such instances, communication is prevented from happening. In a more serious light, if you want to get honest feedback from employees, and you do not want them to just shower accolades hiding their true thoughts, instead of communicating genuinely, you have to find a way that they can communicate, maybe anonymously that would bring about honest feedback. Another interference to communication is **filters** when we hear what we want to hear from a conversation based on our experiences. For example, someone compliments you about something, but because the object of the compliment has been something you have been insecure about for a long time, you are bound to believe such compliments as mere words. The receiver will hear the opposite of what the sender is saying because of their insecurities – filters, or it can be the other way around when an area of improvement is being communicated to you, but you hear it as a compliment because the sender had initially complimented you about something. In such cases, the point is missed and the area of improvement is ignored because the receiver did not understand the message as it was delivered because they filtered it to suit their preferred communication.

How to Ensure Effective Communication
One of the ways to ensure effective communication is to **take time to communicate.** Do not be in a hurry to get the words out. **Explain what you are trying to communicate, listen actively for feedback,** then **let your actions be equivalent to your words.** No mixed messaging; do not say something and then do the opposite. **Be receiver-oriented,** let your communication be structured/directed/tailored to the receiver, and aim to receive an understanding. You have to design communication in a way that the person that is going to receive it understands it. Be accepting of others; no slang or jargon. Accept that other people may not necessarily understand that jargon, then get timely feedback just to ensure that the communication you have passed out is fully understood before too much time passes. **Separate the receiver from the issue/message;** no A-type conflict. Do not fight the person that you are passing information to or the person that is giving you the information. Focus on the issue. That is how to ensure effective communication. **Recognize cultural differences**. Do not make references that those from other cultures may not understand. Finally,

speak clearly and slowly so that people can hear and get the gist of what you are saying, even if they don't get it the first time, by speaking slowly, they will have time to catch up to the understanding.

How to Improve Communication Channels

360-degree feedback - getting feedback from all concerned parties, all stakeholders that you can think of, is 360-degree feedback. **Employee surveys** - get employees to express their opinions. **Suggestion systems** - make it possible for employees to share their ideas as well. Create **speak-up programs,** maybe anonymously, making it possible for everyone throughout the organization to speak up when things are not going right. If they feel like they are being victimized, let them speak up, without retaliation or fear of one. **Open door policy** - let there not be any barrier between employees and leadership of the organization. Let employees know that they can walk up to the leaders and express themselves. **Hotlines** - create avenues that if something urgent is happening, there is a channel of communication, that information can be disseminated straightaway for the right action to be taken in response. **Intranet** - intracompany-wide information that is available to those within that organization, so even if there is no one around when an employee has a question. The information is there for them to search for it and find answers to the immediate issue before they find anyone else to ask. **Webcast** - web meetings, regular meetings broadcasted by video or information dissemination sessions like town halls, via the web. **Presentation** - demonstrating information to the team/ employees. Having **roundtable** discussions as well can improve communication channels.

I hope that we have been able to link these headings - organizational culture, team dynamics, employee engagement, organization structure, and communication to the importance of aligning organization strategy, processes, structure, and job design, the organizations' personality (Culture) with human resources practices. Organizational culture feeds into strategy, and strategy needs employees to support it to succeed. If there is a gap, there is a need for a culture change, and the need to carry everyone along – communication – and ultimately for the organization to meet its goal, which is why organizations exist.

www.ingramcontent.com/pod-product-compliance
Lightning Source LLC
Chambersburg PA
CBHW030506220526
45464CB00006B/2679